Baby Animals

SCHOLASTIC INC.
New York Toronto London
Auckland Sydney Mexico City
New Delhi Hong Kong

In the jungle

Orangutan

I am orange and fluffy!
I like swinging around
in the trees.

swing swing!

Froglets

Our round, sticky toes help us **cling** to leaves and branches.

Croak croak!

Tapir

My spots and stripes _{hide} me in the jungle. When it gets hot, I go for a swim—splash!

Snuffle snuffle!

Lemur

Every morning,
I *sunbathe* with my
friends. When I want
my mom, I yelp!

Yelp
yelp!

Elephant

Look how **dirty** I am!
I have been wallowing
in mud to keep cool.

Trrrumpet!

Gorilla

My **thick**, woolly coat of black hair covers my whole body—except my face, hands, and feet.

Grunt grunt!

Tiger

I am a tiger cub—grrrr!
I have orange fur with
black **stripes**, and look
at my long whiskers!

zzz zzz zzz!

ISBN 978-0-545-39341-6

12 11 10 9 8 7 6 5 4 3 2   11 12 13 14 15 16/0

Printed in the U.S.A.   40

First Scholastic printing, September 2011

Photo Credits
Every care has been taken to trace copyright holders.

Cover, 1: Press Association/LANDOV; 2 Shutterstock/Eric Isselee;
3 Science Photolibrary/Art Wolfe; 4 Shutterstock/A Cotton Photo; 5 Photolibrary;
6 Getty/James Balog; 7 Corbis/How Hwee Young; 8 Shutterstock/Eric Isselee;
9 Alamy/Val Duncan/Kennebec Images; 10 Alamy/Huw Jones;
11 Frank Lane Picture Agency (FLPA) Martin B. Withers;
12 Nature Picture Library/Suzi Eszterhas; 13 FLPA/Suzi Eszterhas/Minden;
14 Photolibrary/White; 15 Press Association/LANDOV